When Healing Doesn't Come Easily

When Healing Doesn't Come Easily

by Lynne Hammond

Harrison House
Tulsa, Oklahoma

When Healing Doesn't Come Easily
ISBN 1-57794-271-X
Copyright © 2000 by Lynne Hammond
P.O. Box 29469
Minneapolis, MN 55429

Published by Harrison House, Inc.
P. O. Box 35035
Tulsa, Oklahoma 74153

Contents

Introduction

No *Legal* Right

Have you ever heard of a case in which someone found innocent in a court of law was sent to prison anyway and punished for a crime he *did not* commit?

Certainly not! The very idea is absurd. No honest court would allow such an injustice. And no innocent man would stand for it.

Yet, spiritually speaking, many Christians find themselves in that very situation every day. They wake up in the morning to bodies wracked with sickness and pain, to minds burdened with depression and torment. They spend their days suffering punishments inflicted by the Devil in payment for sin.

The fact, however, is that these people aren't sinners. They are born-again, Spirit-filled believers. They love the Lord. They read their Bibles.

The Devil is extracting from them a payment they do not owe. But they pay it anyway because they don't understand their rights and privileges in Jesus. They don't realize that God Himself has declared them innocent in the courtroom of heaven and that therefore the Devil has no legal right to punish them anymore.

The Bible says faith comes by hearing and hearing by the Word of God. (Rom. 10:17.) Until we hear what Jesus did to purchase our healing, we will not have the faith necessary to receive it. We will continue to take the punishment of sickness, even though we have been declared innocent in the courtroom of heaven.

Let's dig into the Word of God and find out what our Advocate, Jesus Christ, has done for us. Let's discover the rights and privileges of being the sons and daughters of God, and from this day forward, let us allow the blood of Jesus to defend our right to divine healing.

Chapter 1

Whose *Report* Will You Believe?

Years ago, my husband, Mac, and I ministered in Russia. One night as Mac was preaching, he asked the Russian congregation an interesting question. He said, "Why do you believe what you believe?"

It made me wonder how many Christians—not just in Russia but here in America as well—would have a solid answer to that question.

Later, I was on the streets in Russia. I ran across a precious elderly lady and asked her the same question: "Why do you believe what you believe?"

"Well..." she began uncertainly.

I told her that I believed the Bible.

"Well, I don't know whether I believe the Bible or not," she faltered. "I believe my priest."

Why Do You Believe?

That is the way many Christians are. Some of us believe what our grandmas said. Others of us may have had friends or relatives who took the time to sit down with us and expound on a few ideas and thoughts, so in our minds we decided, *That's interesting. I think I'll believe that way.*

The problem is, beliefs based on what grandma said or what anybody else said don't have any power. It's what the Bible says that has power. So as Christians, we should believe what we believe because of the Bible.

Unfortunately, however, many people who have been Christians for a long time—people who have studied the Word of God and should be able to teach it to other people—do not really know what the Bible says about subjects like healing. They don't know how to find the Scriptures that talk about Jesus' dying to heal us and pay for our sins. And those same people often wonder why they can't seem to get healed.

Romans 10:17 says faith comes by hearing and hearing by the Word of God. So if we want faith for healing, we need to hear and understand what the Word of God says about it. We need to hear and understand what Jesus did as far as our healing is concerned.

It's not enough just to know the Scriptures about it. We must also *understand* them before we can believe them and receive the blessings they offer us.

Look at Mark 11:23, for example:

> **Whosoever shall say unto this mountain, Be thou removed, and be thou cast into the sea; and shall not doubt in his heart, but shall believe that those things which he saith shall come to pass; he shall have whatsoever he saith.**

You probably know that Scripture, and you may even have it memorized. But do you truly understand and believe it? If you do, it's more than a Bible verse to you. It's a powerful truth that changes your life.

If you understand that Scripture, if you truly believe those things that you say shall come to pass, you put a watch over your mouth. You remove from your vocabulary little clichés like "I'm so sick and tired," "I just could have died" and "I thought I'd go crazy."

That's always the way it is. In fact that's one way you can tell whether or not you truly believe any Scripture. The moment you understand and believe a word from God, it begins to make a difference in your life.

Joy and Peace in Believing

There are also some other evidences or indications of faith. The apostle Paul mentions them in Romans 15:13, where he says:

Now the God of hope fill you with all joy and peace in believing.

Paul prays that we be filled with joy and peace in our believing. So we see right here that if you are believing, or if you are in faith, you have joy and peace.

Suppose you were to talk to someone or witness to someone who was having financial difficulties. Faith comes by hearing, doesn't it? So you begin to preach to him: My God shall supply all of your needs according to his riches in glory. [Phil. 4:19.] He has given you all things that pertain to life and to godliness. [2 Peter 1:3.] Let the Lord be magnified continually who takes pleasure in the prosperity of His servant. [Ps. 35:27.]

You can tell if that person understands and believes those Scriptures by the expression on his face after you have given them to him. If he is still sad, and his mouth is all turned down, and he's still crying, is he in faith? No. How do we know he is not? The Bible says, **The God of hope fill you with all joy and peace in your believing.** So if he is believing the report, he is going to be happy. He is going to be filled with joy and peace.

What Do You Value?

I have noticed something interesting about real believing. People who believe the Word of God esteem it highly; they value it. The Word is very significant in their lives.

There is a definite connection between esteeming and believing. And we certainly know there is a connection between believing and receiving. The people in Jesus' own hometown did not put any value on His words or on the Word of God. Referring to these people, Jesus said, **A prophet is not without honour, but in his own country and among his own kin, and in his own house** (Mark 6:4). The result of their dishonoring Him and God's Word was that, except for healing a few sick folk, Jesus could do no mighty works in their midst. (v. 5.)

Many people do not esteem the Word of God. They do not value it highly. Even Christians, people who love Jesus, often do not value and esteem the Word. For example, I often deal with Christians who have been fighting the good fight of faith but have

12

received evil reports, such as diagnoses of terminal illnesses. I minister to these folks, and I say to them: "We have a healing class on Monday nights for people, like you, who need healing in their bodies. The Bible says the Word of God is what sets you free, and so if you are seeking God for healing, you certainly need the Word of God in your life. You should go to healing class to be filled with God's Word on healing."

Later, when I speak to one of the pastors who leads the healing class on Monday nights, however, and ask him if these people have been in healing class, he says, "No, they haven't been there." Weeks later, I ask again. "No, they've never come," he informs me.

By their complacency, those people prove that they do not esteem and value the Word of God. They just don't believe it is going to do that much good. They don't believe in the importance of it. Do you see how believing and esteeming the Word of God go hand in hand?

How Highly Do You Esteem God's Word?

Where there are believers who esteem God's Word, there is God's miracle-working power.

I saw a firsthand example of esteeming the Word in 1986, when I went to Russia to minister in a miracle crusade. There was no freedom of religion in Russia at that time, so we had to work with the underground. Each night we slipped into a car and the driver dropped us off at the railroad tracks, which we walked down for about a half-mile. Then, in the pitch-black dark, a man who could speak neither English nor Russian picked us up in a black car. He drove us to a house far out in the country.

The house was probably about 1200 square feet. When we went inside, people were so jam-packed shoulder to shoulder that I couldn't even put my purse down beside me.

There were four of us there to minister, and we preached for about six hours straight during the first session. We just had to take a break to eat. We had brought in teaching videos; and so while we ate, those folks, who were still standing, watched the videos.

There were people in that meeting who had been in a prayer group in Siberia. Jesus had appeared to a woman in the prayer meeting and said that there would be a meeting in this house at this time. He told her that some Americans would come to preach there and that they should go.

So they came over 1000 miles to that meeting. They were able to take a train part of the way, but they still had to travel many days on foot. Many times in America you can't even get people to walk across the parking lot in order to hear the Word. This prayer group from Siberia, however, esteemed the Word of God so much that they were willing to walk for days to hear God's ministers speaking it to them!

Recently we returned to Russia. This visit was quite different. Even though by American standards Russia is still far from free, it now claims to have religious freedom. Thus, this time we did not have to use the underground. Instead we rolled in on buses, waving to everyone. We even waved good-bye to the guards as we crossed the border.

Still, in these meetings, there was standing room only along the back. For nearly three hours, people stood. On the last night, even the aisles were full. I wonder how many of us value the Word of God enough to stay through an entire service, standing in the lobby and along the outside walls to listen.

Believe His Report, Receive His Power

With that said, let's make a solid commitment to esteem, understand and believe the Word of God. And let's launch out and see what it says about healing. We'll start with one of the most powerful passages in the Bible—Isaiah 53.

There, the prophet Isaiah, caught up in the Spirit many years in his future, saw what Jesus would one day do for us on the Cross. Many theologians call this "the great substitutionary chapter" because it speaks of how Jesus would eventually take our place by taking upon Himself our sin and the punishment for it.

Isaiah begins this chapter by asking:

> **Who hath believed our report? and to whom is the arm of the Lord revealed?**
>
> **Isaiah 53:1**

Many times we want to rush past this verse to get to the next verses. But let's take a closer look at this. The writer here is asking two questions.

Isaiah first asks, **Who hath believed our report?** In other words, the prophet asks, "Who has believed our message?" What

15

message is he speaking of? The message he is about to give concerning Jesus.

The second question is this: **To whom is the arm of the Lord revealed?** And the answer is clear: The arm of the Lord is revealed to the person who will believe the message.

What is the arm of the Lord? It is the manifested power of God.

In the Old Testament many times you will see something like, "And the hand of God came upon some prophet, judge or king, and he began to prophesy." In 1 Kings 18 we see Elijah on Mount Carmel calling down fire from heaven and inciting a major victory over the prophets of Baal, and the explanation given for the mighty miracles that happened through Elijah that day was that the hand of the Lord came upon him. (v. 46).

When God's power manifests, things change—miracles happen. So when we believe the message, we receive God's power, and things begin to change in our lives to line up with that message.

To whom is the arm of the Lord revealed? To whoever will believe the message we are about to read. So as you read this message, believe God's Word to you and say in your heart, **The arm of the Lord is being revealed to me because I believe.**

A Tender Plant

Now let's look at Isaiah's message. Let's examine the report he gave about Jesus. He said:

For he shall grow up before him as a tender plant, and as a root out of dry ground: he hath no form nor comeliness; and when we shall see him, there is no beauty that we should desire him.

Isaiah 53:2

Here Isaiah compares Jesus' growing up from childhood to adulthood to that of a tender plant.

When my children were in kindergarten, at one point they were studying seeds. Each one of my children grew a little plant and brought it home. (I'm sure many of you who are parents have had this experience.) This plant was very small; it was the most emaciated looking thing. It was just a little stalk with a few leaves on it. It looked so frail—as though if you thumped it, it would have drooped over and died right there.

I was thinking about that in the light of Jesus. Isaiah says that Jesus grew up before the Father **as a tender plant, and as a root out of dry ground.** I think this metaphorical comparison between Jesus and a tender plant is very interesting. A tender plant has no resources of its own. It can neither obtain nor maintain life flow on its own. It depends entirely on external sources of nourishment for its survival. In the same way, Jesus, in His human form, was powerless. Jesus said, **I do nothing of myself; but as my Father hath taught me, I speak these things** (John 8:28).

It also said in Isaiah 53:2, **He hath no form nor comeliness; and when we shall see him, there is no beauty that we should desire him.** That just means there wasn't any particular thing about Jesus' physical appearance that revealed that He was the Son of God. He just looked like another natural man. You would not have seen Him walking down the street and exclaimed,

"Wow! Look at Him! He's the Son of God!" just because of His natural features.

If the people in Jesus' day had seen Him as anything other than a natural man, they could not have tortured and crucified Him.

Jesus Was Despised and Rejected for Us

In Isaiah 53:3-4, Isaiah foretells Jesus' work on the Cross.

He is despised and rejected of men; a man of sorrows, and acquainted with grief: and we hid as it were our faces from him; he was despised, and we esteemed him not.

Surely he hath borne our griefs, and carried our sorrows: yet we did esteem him stricken, smitten of God, and afflicted.

Today when we look at the Cross, we tend to glorify and magnify the object itself. For example, some people wear cross pendants as jewelry; others hang crosses on their walls. But back in the time when Isaiah wrote this passage, the cross was not an object of beauty; it was an instrument of torture and death. It was like the modern-day gas chamber, electric chair or lethal injection. If someone had used a cross as an ornament then, it would have been the same as your wearing a miniature of an electric chair around your neck or hanging a replica of a gas chamber on your wall today.

Crucifixion was reserved for the worst of the worst—the murderers and serial killers. So what we are reading about here is not a glorious scene. It was terrible. Isaiah 53:3 says that all of the people who stood around just to watch Jesus' crucifixion "esteemed him not." They despised, rejected and forsook Him. Men hid their faces from Him. They neither appreciated His worth nor esteemed Him. The soldiers spit on Him, slapped Him, flogged Him, scourged Him. They treated Him like the scum of the earth. Anyone who died this way lost all honor and dignity—and so did his entire family.

Yet this is the way the Master died. There was no one standing around praising God or thanking Him for taking care of sin and sickness for our sake. On the contrary, despite the fact that a crucifixion was so degrading that you normally would not see a leader there, even the religious, political and military leaders were out there to mock Jesus. "Oh you aren't so big now, are you?" they would say. "If you are who you say you are, why don't you come down? Look at him now. He trusted God." (Luke 23:35-37.) And of course, the people saw the Pharisees and the Sadducees there, so they thought Jesus to be the most terrible, wicked man who ever lived.

We know that a few disciples, including John, were there. And we know Jesus' mother, Mary, was there. (John 19:25-27.) And we imagine that they were grieved and confused. But to the majority of the people standing by, Jesus was no more than a criminal worthy of God's wrath.

Jesus Was Cursed for Us

Isaiah 53:4 says, **Yet we did esteem him stricken, smitten of God, and afflicted.** The people standing by as Jesus hung on the Cross believed that God had judged Him, afflicted Him, smote

Him, struck Him. Otherwise, they reasoned, God would not have allowed this to happen.

What they did not realize was that Jesus was bearing the punishment for *their* sins, not His own. Galatians 3:13 says: **Christ hath redeemed us from the curse of the law, being made a curse for us: for it is written, Cursed is every one that hangeth on a tree.**

Think about that for a moment. Jesus took upon Himself the sin of all mankind and the punishment for that sin, which was sickness and disease. Actually, many people are not even aware that sickness is a form of punishment. That is because the Devil has worked feverishly to keep that truth from us. In fact, he has tried to convince us that sickness is a blessing in disguise. He has used religious tradition to teach us that illness is, at times, God's will for us and that we can glorify Him by bearing it without complaint.

Nothing could be further from the truth! Throughout the Word of God, sickness is always referred to as a curse—never a blessing. What is a curse? We know that a curse is bad and that it is evil. A curse is punishment for breaking God's law. It is punishment for rebellion and disobedience. Poverty is punishment. Mental illness is punishment. Oppression and depression are punishment. Destruction is punishment. Sickness and disease are punishment. These are all part of the curse.

If sickness were a blessing, God would have "blessed" Adam and Eve with it in the Garden of Eden. But God only put good things in that garden—and sickness isn't good!

On the contrary, sickness is a part of the evil that came upon the earth when mankind rebelled against God and broke His law.

The Bible leaves no doubt about that. In Deuteronomy 28, God spells out in detail the curse of sin, *including every sickness and every affliction.* (v. 61.)

So we know that when Jesus was cursed for us, the curse He bore included sickness and disease. Isaiah 53:5 says it this way: **But he was wounded for our transgressions, he was bruised for our iniquities: the chastisement of our peace was upon him; and with his stripes we are healed.**

There are many places in the Bible where we could see that the words *beating, scourging, flogging* and *punishment* are all synonymous. Think for a moment about those stripes Jesus bore. Think what an awful sound the cracking of the whip must have made as it tore the skin from His back. Thirty-nine lashes He took for us. It was not a random number, for research reveals there are thirty-nine causes of disease. Thus, with each stripe, Jesus bore those causes so we could go free.

The Price Is Paid

Isaiah, seeing into the spirit, described Jesus' substitutionary work on the Cross in this way:

All we like sheep have gone astray, we have turned every one to his own way; and the Lord has made to light upon Him the guilt and iniquity of us all. He was oppressed, [yet when] He was afflicted, He was submissive and opened not His mouth; like a lamb that is led to the slaughter, and as a sheep before her shearers is dumb, so He opened not his mouth.

By oppression and judgment He was taken away; and as for His generation, who among them considered that He was cut off out of the land of the living [stricken to His death] for the transgression of my [Isaiah's] people, to whom the stroke was due?

And they assigned Him a grave with the wicked, and with a rich man in His death, although He had done no violence, neither was any deceit in His mouth. Yet it was the will of the Lord to bruise Him; He has put Him to grief and made Him sick. When You and He make His life an offering for sin [and He has risen from the dead, in time to come], He shall see His [spiritual] offspring, He shall prolong His days, and the will and pleasure of the Lord shall prosper in His hand.

He shall see [the fruit] of the travail of His soul and be satisfied; by His knowledge of Himself [which he possesses and imparts to others] shall My [uncompromisingly] righteous One, My servant, justify many and make many righteous (upright and in right standing with God), for He shall bear their iniquities and their guilt [with the consequences, says the Lord].

Therefore will I divide Him a portion with the great [kings and rulers], and He shall divide the spoil with the mighty, because He poured out his life unto death, and [He let Himself] be regarded as a criminal and be numbered with the transgressors; yet He bore [and took away] the sin of many and made intercession for the transgressors the rebellious.

Isaiah 53:6-12 AMP

Spiritual and Physical Redemption

It is important to realize all that is happening here, not only naturally but also spiritually. Redemption is both physical and spiritual, because the spiritual is what affects the physical realm. It is true that in this passage we see Jesus dying on the Cross, naturally. We see Him being flogged and scourged. But there is so much more here that we cannot see—things that are happening spiritually.

For instance, Isaiah 52:14 says, **His visage** [appearance] **was so marred more than any other man.** I have heard people preach on that and talk about how mutilated He was. But I don't believe Isaiah is just talking about Jesus' physical condition here.

He couldn't be, because there are people who have been physically marred much more than Jesus was. There are people who have been torn apart in automobile accidents, people who have been mangled in all kinds of machinery accidents and other things. Yet John 19:33-36 says that not a single bone in Jesus' body was broken. So I believe that Isaiah was seeing Jesus' spirit being marred as it took on the horror of the sins of all mankind.

In Mark 14:32-42, we find another indication that more was happening spiritually than naturally in Jesus' sacrifice. In this passage we find Jesus in Gethsemane praying to the Father about His impending death. Sweating blood and crying, He said, **Abba, Father, all things are possible unto thee; take away this cup from me: nevertheless not what I will, but what thou wilt** (Mark 14:36).

Was He doing this because of all the physical pain He would experience? No, that couldn't have been the reason. After all, many of the disciples of Christ were also eventually crucified and, instead of cowing from it, they rejoiced. So if it were true that Jesus was agonizing about the physical pain He would endure, we would have to say that His followers were seemingly more courageous than He was. I don't believe that is true.

So we see Jesus crying out because of something far greater, far worse, than what we can see in the natural. I believe this was the greatest cause of His anguish: He was about to be separated from God the Father, and He was about to take upon His spirit all of the guilt, condemnation and sin of the world.

So we must understand that redemption is first of all spiritual. The spiritual realm then affects the mental and physical realms.

What Are Griefs? Sorrows? Pains?

Jesus died so that your spirit would be made righteous and that your physical body would be healed and remain healthy. We need to look more closely at some of the words in Isaiah 53:3-4, so that we may better understand that, just as forgiveness of sin is part of the Atonement, so is healing.

Verse 4 says, **Surely he hath borne our griefs.** In the original text, we find that the word *grief* is the word *choliy*.[1] This word is also used in reference to every sickness and every disease in the curse in Deuteronomy 28:61, which says, **Also every sickness** [choliy], **and every plague, which is not written in the book of this law, them will the Lord bring upon thee, until thou be destroyed.** So when we read, **Surely he hath borne our griefs,** we are reading, "Surely he hath borne our *sickness and diseases.*"

Now let's look at the word *borne*. In the original text, the word translated *borne* is the Hebrew word *nasa*, and it means "to lift, carry, take."[2] So we could read that phrase this way: "Surely He lifted, took and carried our sicknesses and diseases upon Himself."

The next part of that verse says, **...and carried our sorrows.** The word in the original text for sorrow is *makob*, which means "pain."[3] This word is also used in reference to Job's sufferings: **He is chastened also with pain** [makob] **upon his bed, and the multitude of his bones with strong pain** [makob] (Job 33:19). So, speaking of Jesus, we could say, "Surely He has borne our sickness and carried our pain."

Young's Literal Translation interprets verses 3-4 this way:

He is despised, and left of men, a man of pains and acquainted with sickness. And as one hiding the face from us, he is despised, and we esteemed him not. Surely our sicknesses he hath borne, and our pains—he hath carried them, and we—we have esteemed him plagued, smitten of God and afflicted.[4]

The following translations of Isaiah 53:4 reinforce this interpretation.

The Leeser translation says, **Yet it was our pains that he bore and our sorrows that he carried.**[5]

The *J.P.S. Translation*, which is a Jewish translation, says, **Surely our diseases He did bare and our pains He carried.**[6]

The *New American Standard Bible* says, **Surely our griefs** [sickness] **He Himself bore, and our sorrows** [pains] **He carried.**

The *New English Bible* says, **Yet on Himself He bore our sufferings and our torments He endured.**

Is This Message for Us Today?

Now, I have had people say to me, "Sister, this is an Old Testament Scripture. Where does it talk about this in the New Testament?" The apostle John says:

> **But though [Jesus] had done so many miracles before them, yet they believed not on him: that the saying of Esaias the prophet might be fulfilled, which he spake, Lord, who hath believed our report? and to whom hath the arm of the Lord been reveled? Therefore they could not believe, because that Esaias said again, He hath blinded their eyes, and hardened their heart; that they should not see with their eyes, nor understand with their heart, and be converted, and I should heal them.**
>
> **John 12:37-40**

This Scripture passage is about Jesus. It recalls Isaiah's foretelling of the miracles and healings Jesus would perform by God's extended arm. (Isa. 53:1.) John 12:41 says, **These things said Esais when he saw his [Jesus'] glory, and spake of him.** Jesus fulfilled Isaiah's prophecy. He became our Savior and our Healer. And John echoes Isaiah's words in the New Testament, letting us know that those who believe that report about the Messiah will be healed—and those who don't, won't.

No Long Faces, Please!

Paul also quotes Isaiah's reference to believing God's report about Jesus' saving, healing work on the Cross. In Romans 10:15-17 he says:

> **As it is written, How beautiful are the feet of them that preach the gospel of peace, and bring glad tidings of good things! But they have not all obeyed the gospel. For [Isaiah] saith, Lord, who hath believed our report? So then faith cometh by hearing, and hearing by the Word of God.**

So we see here that Paul connects hearing and believing and faith with Isaiah 53:1.

Think again about what that verse said. It said that if we believe the report about Jesus and His healing, atoning work on the Cross, we will see the arm of the Lord extended in our lives. We will experience the mighty, miracle-working power of God.

Paul understood something about what that power can do. That's why in Ephesians 1:19-21 AMP, Paul, praying for the Church, says:

> **And [so that you can know and understand] what is the immeasurable and unlimited and surpassing greatness of His power in and for us who believe, as demonstrated in the working of His mighty strength, which He exerted in Christ when He raised Him from the dead and seated Him at His [own] right hand in the heavenly [places], far above all rule and authority and power and dominion and every name that is named [above every title that can be conferred], not only in this age and in**

**the world, but also in this age and in this world, but also
in the age and world which are to come.**

Can you even begin to imagine the power it took to raise Jesus from the dead? He had taken upon Himself the sin of all mankind in the past, present and future. He had borne all sickness and all diseases for us. So the Father had to exert His mighty power to get through that barrier of sin, sickness, disease and death standing between Jesus and Himself.

God rolled up His sleeves and extended His arm to raise Jesus from hell, from sin, from the grave and from sickness and disease with an explosion of supernatural power the likes of which the world had never seen. Then He exalted Him "above all rule and authority and power and dominion."

Will you believe the report? If so, you'll see the arm of the Lord at work in you!

Chapter 2

Don't Just *Stand* There—
Say Something!

As we discovered in chapter 1, God's report is that Jesus bore our sicknesses and carried our pains. It is important that if you believe this report, you speak it, because according to 2 Corinthians 4:13, the spirit of faith speaks!

When you say what God says, the Holy Ghost—the Spirit of truth—connects with the truth spoken from your mouth. And just as the Holy Spirit moved on the Word God spoke in Genesis 1 and brought it to pass, He will move on the Word of God that you speak and He will bring it to pass. When God said, "Light be!" the Holy Spirit, the power arm of the Godhead, caused light to explode into being. And when you say, "By His stripes I am healed" that same Spirit will make you whole!

People have said to me, "Well, Sister, I tried that, and it didn't work." If it didn't, then you weren't believing when you said it. So you need to keep saying it until you believe. I remember in 1972, I must have confessed this Scripture 1000 times a day. If you keep saying it and meditating on it, you will believe the report.

To whoever will believe the report that Jesus carried our sickness and pain, the arm of the Lord is revealed. If you will believe and speak this report, then God's promise of healing will manifest in your life.

He Already Carried Them

Sadly enough, religious folks sometimes decline that promise. With a false sense of humility they say things like, "Oh, God has already done enough for me. I won't ask Him to heal me. I'll just try to bear this pain gracefully. I'll just try to glorify God in my suffering."

That's silly. If Jesus bore your sickness and carried your pains, oppression and so forth, you don't have to bear them. Why would Jesus bear them if He wanted you to bear them once again?

If I had a great big box that was too heavy for me to carry and I got a strong man to carry it from the house to the car for me, would I then carry the box back into the house, saying, "I have to carry that again"? Of course I wouldn't. That would mean that man's work was in vain.

So, if Jesus already carried sickness, pain and oppression for us, why would we carry it again? If Jesus loved us so much that He suffered all that He suffered, took all that He took, carried all that He carried and bore all that He bore, why do we think it would bring Him any glory for us to carry it again?

We need to wake up to the benefits of Jesus' sacrifice for us. Otherwise, we make His work for us in vain.

Not for Hire

As I was driving down the highway thinking about that fact some time ago, I saw a big eighteen-wheel truck with a sign on it that read, "Not for Hire." Do you know what that sign meant? It meant that trucker was not willing to carry anyone else's stuff. He only carried the stuff that belonged to the owner of his company. So you might as well not call and ask him to carry your stuff, because he won't do it.

As Christians, we ought to have that same sign on us in the realm of the spirit: "Not for Hire." And when the Devil comes around trying to load us with sickness and depression and condemnation, we ought to refuse it and say, "Get out of here, Devil. I'm not carrying that stuff. Jesus carried it for me 2000 years ago, and I'm not carrying it again!"

Some of you reading this just need to get absolutely indignant. Refuse to be the Devil's pack mule or to bear his stuff. Jesus bore that junk once and for all, and you don't have to bear it!

You say, "Well, I still have these symptoms in my body." Yes, you may have symptoms in your body, and I realize you cannot blink your eyes and make those symptoms disappear. You need to realize, though, that those symptoms' being in your body does not mean they have to be in your heart.

You never, ever have to *receive* them. You never have to give in and say, "I guess I'll just agree with these symptoms instead of the Word of God. These symptoms tell me I'm sick, so I guess I'll just have to be sick." No, you can say, "Symptoms or no symptoms, I'm going to agree with the Word. The Word says I'm healed, so I am."

You don't have to agree with the doctor's negative report, either. I have heard of people the doctors describe as *carriers* of some virus or genetic deficiency. If a doctor says that to you, just remember that Jesus already carried that sickness or disease, so you don't have to.

Mathew 8:17 says, **Himself took our infirmities, and bare our sicknesses.** Do not let Jesus' redemptive work be in vain. Receive your healing as done. It is done! Jesus has already done everything that He is going to do about your healing. He bore your sicknesses, and He carried your pain. He did it that day on the Cross at Calvary. He has already done it. It is finished.

Open Your Mouth and Enforce the Law

So if you are reading this and you have symptoms in your body, whatever they might be, you can lift your hand to the Father right now in the name of Jesus. Do it right now. First, name whatever it is that is attacking you. It may be cancer, for example. In a strong, authoritative voice, say, "Cancer, I'm talking to you! Cancer, you leave me now. You have no right to be in my body. Jesus already carried you, so I don't have to. You get out of my body. You leave me, in the name of Jesus. The name of Jesus is higher than the name of cancer. I am healed!"

Maybe it is depression that you are dealing with. Say, "You leave me, depression. You can't stay in my body. You can't stay in my mind. No, you are not coming to my house. You get off these premises. In the name of Jesus Christ, I take authority over you. I have perfect peace in my mind!"

That is the way you have to talk to the Devil, and that is the way you have to take what is rightfully yours.

Say it all day long. "No, sickness, you are not coming here. You leave me, in the name of Jesus. You get out of my body. You leave my household."

Maybe you've been dealing with financial bondage. You say, "Bondage, leave me! You are not welcome here. I have been made free by the blood of Jesus!"

So, you see, we are constantly reinforcing Satan's defeat. He is already defeated, but you have to enforce that defeat. Why? Because Satan is an outlaw. Even though it's spiritually illegal for him to put the curse of sickness on a child of God, he'll do it anyway if he can get away with it.

You can understand that if you'll think about the work of a policeman. There are laws in the land that we are to abide by. Some people, however, will break those laws, so policemen are out there to enforce those laws. Similarly, we must enforce our victory over Satan and the curse.

A Legion of Angels To Defend Us

We enforce that victory with the words of our mouth.

You might be thinking, *Are words really that powerful?* They are when they are words of truth spoken in Jesus' name. That's why Jesus kept quiet when Judas betrayed Him into the hands of the religious leaders just before His crucifixion.

If you've read the account of what happened there in the Garden of Gethsemane, you will recall that when they were about to take Jesus off to be crucified, Peter whipped out his sword and cut off the ear of the chief priest's servant. How did Jesus respond? He turned to Peter and said, "Put your sword up, for I could call more than twelve legions of angels. But then how would the Scripture be fulfilled?" (Matt. 26:52-54.)

Jesus could have called twelve legions of angels to protect and deliver Him, but He didn't. The Bible says, **He was oppressed, and he was afflicted, yet he opened not his mouth** (Isa. 53:7).

You see, Jesus' captors did not have a legal right to take Him. They did not have a legal right to touch Jesus. The Devil only has a legal right to oppress and afflict the guilty, the unrighteous, with sickness, poverty and destruction. He has no legal right to attack the righteous.

Now, I know sickness, poverty and destruction illegally affect a lot of people. But the Devil only has a *legal* right to oppress the sinner, the guilty.

So, did the Devil have a right to send these religious leaders to capture and torment Jesus? No, he did not. Jesus was innocent; He was sinless. This right here is where the Devil overplayed his hand. This is where he lost. This is where he fell right into God's trap. That's why in 1 Corinthians 2:8 Paul says that if they had known what they were doing, they never would have crucified the Lord of glory.

Jesus didn't open His mouth. At any time He could have appealed to the Father on the grounds that he was innocent, spotless, sinless. Just imagine the temptation there. He could have appealed to the Father and said, "Father, I'm innocent. I have done no wrong; I have committed no sin. The Devil has no legal right to touch me." And the Father legally would have had to deliver Him. Is that not right?

But if He had done that, if He had opened His mouth, the blood of Jesus would never have been shed. The plan of redemption would have been aborted. And we would still be lost.

Paul Claimed His Rights

Let me show you a very interesting passage of Scripture in Acts 22 that illustrates how you can enforce natural legal rights simply by opening your mouth and saying something. It's in Acts 22. There we find Paul in a lot of trouble. He was in Jerusalem, about to be killed. The Roman soldiers came out to take him and scourge him.

> **And as they bound him with thongs, Paul said unto the centurion that stood by, Is it lawful for you to scourge a man that is a Roman, and uncondemned?**
>
> **When the centurion heard that, he went and told the chief captain, saying, Take heed what thou doest: for this man is a Roman. Then the chief captain came, and said unto him, Tell me, art thou a Roman? He said, Yea. And the chief captain answered, with a great sum obtained I this freedom. And Paul said, But I was free born.**
>
> **Then straightway they departed from him which should have examined him: and the chief captain also was afraid, after he knew that he was a Roman, and because he had bound him.**
>
> **Acts 22:25-29**

Just as the guards stretched Paul out to flog him, he turned around and said, "Hey, is it legal for you to do this to me? I'm a Roman citizen."

Now, if you were a citizen of Rome back then, you were somebody important. You had legal rights. Nobody could take a Roman citizen to trial without appealing to Caesar. Then that Roman citizen would have to have a fair trial, and he could appeal it all the way back up to Caesar again.

Paul handled this situation by opening his mouth. And when he said, "Hey, you don't have any legal right to do this," they started scurrying around, didn't they? They said, "You won't tell anybody that this happened, will you?" They got really scared. But you see, Paul stopped his scourging. He stopped those soldiers from putting stripes on his back. How did he stop them? He stopped them by opening his mouth; he claimed his rights as a citizen of Rome.

You Are Not Guilty

If you're wondering why this incident is important to you, I'll tell you. It's because Paul is not the only Christian who has been wrongfully accused. According to Revelation 12:10, the Devil comes accusing you day and night.

How should you respond? By the blood of the Lamb and the word of your testimony! (Rev. 12:11.) When Satan starts to scourge you with sickness, you should respond just as Paul did. You should open your mouth and declare your citizenship. You should say, "Look here, Devil, I'm not a citizen of this world. I'm a citizen of the kingdom of God. I was born again into that kingdom by the blood of Jesus. So you don't have any right to put sickness on me!"

Sadly, many people don't do that because they are not always sure they have a right to speak up. After all, we are not perfect. There are times when we sin, times when our failures make us feel unworthy and undeserving of any of God's promises, including healing.

But we should forever dismiss such thoughts. The truth is that as long as we are walking with God and trusting in the blood of Jesus, in God's sight we are absolutely innocent! Jesus took our guilt for us. The gavel of heaven has fallen and judgment has been rendered in our favor. God has pronounced us *not guilty.* Therefore the Devil has no legal right to inflict on us any part of the curse.

Jesus Was Silent So We Could Speak

Isn't that wonderful? As believers, you and I are made the righteousness of God. That means the Devil has no legal right to put sickness or pain on us. If he tries, then we can open our mouths in faith, and God will release His power on our behalf. He will rise up in our defense and send demons scurrying in every direction.

Jesus took all those stripes, was smitten of God, took that beating, was struck—and He didn't open His mouth. The reason He didn't open His mouth was so that you and I could open ours. He was silent so you and I could speak. He suffered so you and I could be healed. He took our punishment so we could be free.

Remember that the next time the Devil ties you to the whipping post and starts beating you with sickness and pain and affliction. Don't just silently submit. Resist him. Remind him that you are a citizen of the kingdom of heaven. Remind him that the blood of Jesus has washed away every accusation ever brought against you. Let him know that if he doesn't get his hands off you, then your Father—almighty God Himself—will see to it that he has more trouble than he can handle.

See, the Devil knows that it's unlawful for him to put sickness, disease and oppression on you. But he's hoping you don't know. If you keep your mouth shut, he will just keep loading it on and dishing it out.

And I've seen people just take it and let him tell them they deserve it. *You know you're a bad Christian. You deserve this,* he says to their minds.

When the Devil comes at you trying to load all of his junk on you, you have to challenge him. Stand up and defy him.

Because of the Blood

Remember, if you are walking with the Lord and have confessed your sin, then you are the righteousness of God—you are innocent through His blood. You are not innocent in your own self. You are not innocent just because you think you're cute or good-looking. You are innocent because of the blood. God sees you through the blood. He's seeing you through the work of redemption. He's seeing you through Jesus. That's how God looks at you.

Now open your mouth and tell the Devil: "Surely He has borne my sickness and carried my pain. I am innocent because of the blood. The Father sees and looks at me through the blood. I've been justified by the blood. God has pronounced blessing upon me, and the curse cannot come in. Jesus took the curse of sickness. He took the curse of poverty. What God has blessed cannot be cursed, in Jesus' name."

Now praise the Lord for your healing because it is already done. Say: "Thank you, Jesus, for taking those stripes on your back so that I can walk free from the curse of sickness. I am healed. Hallelujah!"

Our Victory Is Jesus' Joy

It thrills Jesus when we walk in His Word this way. After all, He paid a high price for our heavenly citizenship. Hebrews 12:2 says that He endured the Cross and all its shame **for the joy that was set before him.** What was that joy? It was the joy of seeing you and me walking free from the curse. It was the joy of seeing us overcoming sin, sickness and the Devil himself **by the blood of the Lamb, and by the word of** [our] **testimony** (Rev. 12:11).

As I said before, if you have symptoms of sickness on your body, I realize you cannot blink and make them disappear. However, there is something you can do. You can refuse to receive that sickness in your heart. You can turn your attention away from the symptoms and onto the Word of God instead.

You can look steadfastly with the eyes of your spirit upon the precious Savior, who bought your healing. You can meditate on what He has done for you until the reality of it overshadows all else and you cry out in joy, "By His stripes, I was healed!" The power of heaven will back those words when you say them in faith. And the Devil will back down. He will flee just as the Bible said he would. (James 4:7.)

The verdict has been given and cannot be reversed. The righteous Judge of all the earth has found you innocent by virtue of the blood of Jesus. He has received the sacrifice on your behalf and declared you forever *not guilty*. The Devil has no legal right to punish you anymore. Open your mouth and claim your right to healing, for you have been set free!

Chapter 3

The *Keys* to Spiritual Fitness

Now, I'm going to be very honest with you. Just because you've asserted your spiritual rights doesn't mean the battle is over. Just because you've risen up in faith and spoken the Word once or twice doesn't mean the Devil will instantly pack up his stuff and go home, never to bother you again. No, the odds are, he'll launch a counterattack against you and try to steal the Word of God about healing that's been planted in your heart. (Mark 4:14-20.)

He may hit you with new symptoms—or a return of the old ones. Then he'll pressure you mentally by bringing you thoughts like, *See, you aren't really healed after all. The Word doesn't work for you as it does for Sister Lynne. You might as well just give up and be sick.*

What do you do when that happens?

You **fight the good fight of faith** (1 Tim. 6:12). You refuse to yield to those thoughts and you hold fast to the Word of God.

To do that, you need a strong spirit. That's why Proverbs 18:14 AMP says:

The strong spirit of a man sustains him in bodily pain or trouble, but a weak and broken spirit who can raise up or bear?

What is going to take you through when the Devil launches a counterattack of sickness, disease, bodily pain or trouble against you? A strong spirit!

Recently someone said to me, "Well, you know, God is sovereign, and whether someone makes it through to victory or not is up to God."

It's true that God is sovereign, but He is not the only one who makes that decision. If He were, everybody would get through because God's Word says He wants everybody well. Colossians 3:25 says that God is no respecter of persons. His Word is for everyone. So we must conclude that if it were left to God alone, everyone would be healed.

There is more to it than just God's sovereign will. To a great extent, your own heart and your own faith determine your outcome. It is with the heart that man believes (Rom. 10:10), so you must strengthen your heart to believe and keep on believing God's promises of healing despite the opposition of the Devil.

Varying Levels of Faith

Strong faith does not come out of a weak spirit. Strong faith is a product of a strong spirit. To many people that's a new idea. They don't realize that their inner man is much like their outward man. It can be robust and powerful, emaciated and powerless, or at varying degrees in between.

Second Corinthians 4:16 AMP bears this out. It says:

> **Though our outer man is [progressively] decaying and wasting away, yet our inner self [our spirit] is being [progressively] renewed day after day.**

If the inner man must be renewed day by day, we can conclude that it can be depleted. So if the spirit can be depleted and renewed, we could conclude that people's spirits are at varying levels of strength. Some are strong; some are weak.

From the Scriptures we have just read, we see that the condition of your spirit determines whether you will be able to resist the Devil and come through trials, overcome temptations and receive your healing from God. Years ago I heard Brother Kenneth E. Hagin say that some Christians are sick because they don't know what belongs to them. Other Christians, he said, are sick because they are too spiritually weak to appropriate healing in their lives. In other words, you must be strong in your spirit to receive from the Lord.

Are You Strong Enough To Receive?

Right before my daddy died, he wanted to read his Bible in his room in the nursing home. Yet he was not physically strong enough to hold on to his Bible. We had to prop it up in front of him, but it still didn't work very well. He did not have the physical strength to take it.

Similarly, you have to be spiritually strong to take whatever God has provided for you. Think about righteousness, for instance. First Corinthians 1:30 says that Jesus is made unto us righteousness.

Then 2 Corinthians 5:21 says that we are the righteousness of God in Christ Jesus. Yet all the time I visit with people who cannot receive their righteousness. They live under a sense of condemnation.

Why can't they receive that righteousness? Why can't they accept that God sees them through the blood Atonement?

The reason is that their spirits are weak.

It is the same with finances. In order to receive what God wants you to have in the financial realm, you have to be spiritually strong enough to receive.

Sin Overtakes the Weak in Heart

In Ezekiel 16, God, speaking through Ezekiel, talked to the Israelites about all the terrible things they had done. They had polluted the altars and were worshipping and sacrificing to idols. They were breaking the laws and the commandments of God, so He said, **How weak is thine heart...seeing thou doest all these things** (v. 30).

You show me an individual who cannot get out of sin, who cannot say no to temptation, and I'll show you a person who is weak in his spirit. Now, I am not necessarily talking about what we, as humans, would consider to be heinous sins, such as perhaps murder or incest. I'm talking about the things that all of us battle on a daily basis.

For example, why can't we pass up the temptation to gossip and to criticize? Why can't we pass up the sins of self-centeredness and selfishness?

Why can't we become spiritually disciplined? Some of us will try for three days to get in a groove of Bible reading and prayer; then on the fourth day we slip up and we are right back where we were before. Why can't we commit ourselves to God and be diligent in the things of God?

It's because our spirits are weak and, therefore, our flesh is always taking charge. This is often the reason why we have trouble reaching out to receive our healing or the other blessings God has provided for us.

Who Is Ruling Whom?

Not long ago, a lady called on the phone and asked me to cast a spirit of slumber out of her. She couldn't seem to get up in the morning.

I said, "Honey, that's not a spirit. That's your flesh. Now, I want to ask you something. Who is ruling whom? Is your body controlling you, or is your spirit controlling your body? From what you are telling me, it sounds as though your spirit, way down inside of you is whispering in a weak, little voice, *You'd better get up. You'd better get up,* but your flesh is over there shouting, *Shut up! We're going to sleep as long as we want to! You be quiet!*

That's what happens in a lot of situations. Consider this scenario, for instance. Your spirit is whispering, *You'd better not have that next piece of pie.* Then your flesh shouts, *Be quiet! I'm going to have three more pieces of pie if I want to.* Then you give in to the hollering flesh.

Does this sound familiar? This is what the Bible describes as carnal Christianity. (Rom. 7:14.)

Do you remember what Paul said on this subject? He said, "I keep my body under." (1 Cor. 9:27.) What part of his being was he talking about when he said *I*? He was talking about his real self, his spirit. He said, "I keep my body under the control of the real me, my spirit."

He then went on to say, **lest that by any means, when I have preached to others, I myself should be a castaway.** Paul knew that no matter how long he walked with the Lord, no matter how many visions he saw or revelations he had or how mature he was, if he let his flesh start ruling him, his ministry would be ruined.

Even Paul, who wrote a great portion of the New Testament and received mighty revelations from God, could have wound up on the spiritual junk-heap with his ministry on the rocks if he had yielded to his flesh. If it could happen to him, it could certainly happen to us.

However, if we strengthen our spirits, they can intimidate our flesh. When your inner man is strong, he will say in a powerful voice, *You'd better not watch TV. You'd better get in there and pray.*

Your flesh may whisper like a little child, *Oh, could we please, please watch TV?*

But your spirit will shout, *Be quiet!* It will dominate your life.

So you can see here how the condition of your spirit will make all the difference in how you will resist the Devil, how you will come through hard times and how you will receive from God everything you need, including healing.

The Magnet

One day I was praying about faith and about giving people instruction on faith, and God gave me an object lesson that helped me see this truth more clearly. He reminded me of an experiment I did in my eighth grade science class.

In this experiment, I had a little tissue filled with little metal particles that looked like grains of sand. I took all of those particles and spread them out on two big sheets of notebook paper.

Next I put a little magnet on that paper, and it pulled a few of those little particles around it. Then I did the same things with progressively larger magnets, and they pulled increasing numbers of particles. The last one was like a big brick. It started pulling in all of those particles before it was even close to the paper.

After God reminded me of this experiment. He said, *Faith is very much like a magnet. The larger and stronger that magnet is, the more it will pull in.*

Faith pulls things from the unseen realm into the seen realm. The stronger your faith, the further you can reach into the spirit realm to pull God's gifts into the physical and mental realms.

Big Truck, Little Truck

Strong faith and a strong spirit go hand in hand. You'll never see a person with a weak spirit have strong faith. Why? Little faith doesn't pull big loads. A little truck won't pull nearly as much as an eighteen-wheeler will. The bigger the truck is and the more powerful its engine is, the bigger the load it's going to pull. In the same way, the stronger your spirit is, the further you are going to be able to reach to take hold of what God has for you in your life.

Nourish and Exercise Your Spirit

How do you develop a strong spirit? The writer of 1 Timothy tells us.

If you lay all these instructions before the brethren, you will be a worthy steward and a good minister of Christ Jesus, ever nourishing your own self on the truths of the faith and of the good [Christian] instruction which you have closely followed.

But refuse and avoid irreverent legends (profane and impure and godless fictions, mere grandmothers' tales) and silly myths, and express your disapproval of them. Train yourself toward godliness (piety), [keeping yourself spiritually fit]. For physical training is of some value (useful for a little), but godliness (spiritual training) is useful and of value in everything and in every way, for it holds promise for the present life and also for the life which is to come.

1 Timothy 4:6-8 AMP

In this passage, physical development parallels spiritual development. We see that just as you can be physically fit, you can be spiritually fit. We also see that the principles involved in building yourself up physically are the same as those in building yourself up spiritually.

To build yourself up physically, the first thing you must do is to nourish your body. You must eat. But you can't eat just anything; you need to eat good food. Most Americans' diets are made up of grease, salt and sugar, none of which are very nourishing to the body.

Similarly, Christians need to drink the pure, unadulterated milk of the Word of God and eat the strong meat of it to properly nourish their spirits. Unfortunately, however, our spiritual diet is often as bad as our physical diet. All too often, we hear frothy and frivolous preaching that is not very conducive to spiritual nourishment. We feed ourselves the junk food of the world— newspapers, magazines and television—much more than we feed on the Word.

Instead, we need to be filling our bodies with healthy food, and filling our souls with good truths of faith and scriptural instructions. We need to be acting on Proverbs 4:20-23 AMP, which says:

> **My son, attend to my words; consent and submit to my sayings. Let them not depart from your sight; keep them in the center of your heart. For they are life to those who find them, healing and health to all their flesh. Keep and guard your heart with all vigilance and above all that you guard, for out of it flow the springs of life.**

Notice this passage says your heart is the fountain of life for your mind and body. In order to have life flowing through your arms, legs, bones and all the parts of your body, that life from God must flow through your heart—your spirit—into the other parts of you. If you need healing, you need life to manifest in you. And that life is going to flow through your spirit to your flesh.

Now, if life can flow through your spirit, sickness and disease can flow through your spirit as well. Sickness and disease can come from the Devil to your spirit through reports contrary to God's report, then to your flesh. But when you fill your heart with the life of God, it dispels that sickness and disease.

Eat!

Several years ago, I was seeking God's wisdom concerning certain areas of healing. At the time, we were praying for several people to be healed and I was overcoming pneumonia myself. I was constantly playing tapes of healing school classes. I also listened to tapes of healing confessions and made the confessions along with the tapes. I had the recording playing at night. Several times, I would pause for a few minutes and say, "Lord, what do you want me to do now?"

He'd say, *Eat!* I thought that was most amazing. I had been eating, but He wanted me to keep eating. *Eat. Eat*, He would say.

So I'd pick up my Bible, and I'd go after it again.

The Holy Ghost always shows you the way of escape. It's not the same every time. The Bible says that man does not live by bread alone but by every word that proceeds from the mouth of God. (Deut. 8:3; Matt. 4:4.) So if we will listen to the Word proceeding from His mouth and do whatever He says, that Word will give us the way of escape.

I've been healed through the laying on of hands fewer than ten times since I started walking with the Lord in 1972. The majority of the times that I've been healed have been the result of my doing Proverbs 4:20-21: attending to His words, not letting them depart from my eyes, keeping them in the midst of my heart. And just as verse 22 says, they've become life and health to me. His Word has become medicine to my body.

During this time, I would spiritually eat and eat and eat God's Word. The Lord said to me, *The enemy is out to do one of two things with you. He's out to either starve you or poison you.* Either one will result in death. Isn't that true? If the Devil can't starve you of the spiritual nourishment of God's Word, then he will try to poison you with errant teaching or reports that are contrary to God's report.

I've heard that Smith Wigglesworth once said that it's no wonder that God's people are so sick: they eat three hot meals a day for their bodies, but spiritually they eat one cold snack a week!

You are not going to get all of the food and all of the nourishment you need by coming to church and reading your Bible once in a while. God's Word must become your daily nourishment.

Read the Label

Wouldn't it be great if God would drop a card out of heaven every day with a nutrition label, like the ones on the backs of cereal boxes, for each of us?

On this label would be the "content" of each of our spirits. I wonder what some people's cards would say. Perhaps one would read, "Twenty-five percent unbelief, 20 percent tradition, 10 percent filler..."

Or wouldn't it be great to have labels on the backs of our books and teaching tapes? I wonder how some of them would rate. Fifteen percent opinion? Twenty-five percent man's ideas?

Well, you know, we can determine our own spiritual content. All we have to do is what the Bible says in Ephesians 5:15-17 AMP:

> **Look carefully then how you walk! Live purposefully and worthily and accurately, not as the unwise and witless, but as wise (sensible, intelligent people), making the very most of the time [buying up each opportunity], because the days are evil. Therefore do not be vague and thoughtless and foolish, but understanding and firmly grasping what the will of the Lord is.**

That is what I call spiritual inventory. Maybe when we get up every morning we should take a spiritual inventory. Maybe we should look carefully at how we're living and ask ourselves what we're filling ourselves full of. Are we full of the Word? Are we full of faith and the joy of the Lord? Or are we full of the world's junk?

Many people never take inventory. They just go through life like this: Get up in the morning, have breakfast, watch the news, go to work, come home, fall asleep and get up the next day.

What's happening to you? Where are you going? What are you doing about your spirit?

We often put a lot of effort into developing ourselves mentally and physically, but what are we doing to develop our spirits? The Bible says that a strong spirit is what is going to take you through every attack; it is what is going to cause you to receive from God your healing and every blessing He is so *desperately* trying to get into your hands.

Taste God's Word

Job said that the ear tries, or tastes, words just as the mouth tastes meat. (Job 34:3.) Psalm 34:8 says, **Taste and see that the Lord is good.** How are you going to taste? With your ears.

Jesus said, **Man shall not live by bread alone, but by every word that proceedeth out the mouth of God** (Matt. 4:4). Jeremiah said, "I found your words and ate them, and they became the joy and rejoicing of my soul." (Jer. 15:16.)

The Devil wants to starve you so you will be weak and your faith will be at a low ebb, because then you will not be able to resist him or receive from God.

You know this. Think about what happens to you when you sit down to read your Bible. Although the telephone hasn't rung all day, it will ring fifteen times when you are trying to read your Bible. You will be distracted 1000 times. The Devil will bring all kinds of interruptions. What is he trying to do? He's trying to starve you of your spiritual nourishment.

So we need to learn to ignore those distractions and eat the Word of God.

In John 6:53, Jesus told us we have no life in us unless we eat His flesh and drink His blood. What was He talking about? The Pharisees thought He was talking about natural things, about cannibalism, and they got mad. But Jesus was talking about a spiritual thing. He was saying that when we accept His work on the Cross, our spirits are filled with His life. Then in verse 63, He said, **The words that I speak unto you, they are spirit, and they are life.**

So, metaphorically speaking, we eat words. We could also say that we eat thoughts, because words are really containers of thoughts. Words are letters assembled together to communicate thoughts. Those words wouldn't mean anything to you if they didn't convey thoughts.

The Bible is a book of God's thoughts, conveyed through His words. If you begin to think His thoughts after Him, you will be feeding your spirit with spiritual substance. The thoughts that come from God's Word into your heart have power and life in them that flow to all the parts of your body.

Words come through your ears when you hear them or through your eyes when you read them. Your mind takes those thoughts down into your spirit, and your spirit digests them and you have nourishment. Then those things become a part of you. You've heard the saying "You are what you eat." This is absolutely true spiritually.

Exercise Increases Strength

Not only must you nourish your spirit with the Word of God, but you must also exercise your spirit if you want it to be strong enough to reach out in faith for your healing.

A good way to understand spiritual strength is to compare it to physical strength. For instance, when you first start working out you may be able to do ten pushups if you exert great effort. But if you keep at it, you can develop your muscles to the point that you can do 100 pushups in a row.

Similarly, when you first get saved, it may be difficult just to believe God for small things. But if you keep developing and exercising your spirit, you can pull the most wonderful things out of the spiritual realm and into the physical and mental realms of your life.

One of the ways we exercise our spirits is through worship. I'm not talking about singing. There is a difference between worship and singing. It's ever so important for you to worship God, rather than merely singing to Him.

Do you know God is a jealous God? He will have no gods between you and Him. (Ps. 78:58.) Through worship, you show God that He alone is your life. He is not first in your life; He is not second in your life. God *is* your life. You wouldn't be here if it weren't for God.

There are many other ways to exercise your spirit and make it strong. One way is by believing. Another way is by confessing the Word. Yet another way is by praying in tongues.

You can also pray for yourself the prayer Paul prayed for the Ephesian church.

May He [the Lord] grant you out of the rich treasury of His glory to be strengthened and reinforced with mighty power in the inner man.... That you may be filled [through all your being] unto all the fullness of

God [may have the richest measure of the divine Presence, and become a body wholly filled and flooded with God Himself]!

Ephesians 3:16,19 AMP

Make Time!

If you want God to intervene in your life and heal your body or your mind, you will have to take time to nourish and exercise your spirit so that you can become spiritually strong. You will have to let God interfere with your schedule.

In 1972, I was hit with mental illness that came in the form of deep depression. It was like cancer of the mind, and the Devil tried to use it to take my life. The way I came through that most demonic, horrendous time in my life was by nourishing and exercising my spirit.

That is the only way any of us will make it through in victory. Remember, sickness and disease work in your body twenty-four hours a day, seven days a week. You can't just get one little spiritual feeding or one little spiritual pushup and flip the Word out and say, "Well, by His stripes I'm healed," once a day and be healed. You will have to eat and exercise.

I'm telling you, church of the Lord Jesus Christ, we've got to become progressively stronger in our spirits. We should never be roller-coaster Christians, going up and down, up and down in our faith. We should be progressively stronger every day.

Say aloud, "I am developing a strong spirit. I am growing day by day. I am being renewed and strengthened in my inner man so that I can resist the Devil, so that I can do the will of God, so that I can fulfill the plan of God for my life. In the name of Jesus. Amen.

Chapter 4

Be *Still* and Know

In order to have a strong spirit that can reach out and receive the healing promises of God, not only must you receive spiritual nourishment and exercise, but you must also rest. Just as your physical body must rest to be healthy, so must your spirit rest. How do you rest spiritually? By waiting on the Lord. Isaiah reveals what happens when we wait on the Lord. He says:

> **Have you not known? Have you not heard? The everlasting God, the Lord, the Creator of the ends of the earth, does not faint or grow weary; there is no searching of His understanding. He gives power to the faint and weary, and to him who has no might He increases strength [causing it to multiply and making it to abound]. Even youths shall faint and shall be weary, and [selected] young men shall feebly stumble and fall exhausted; but those who wait for the Lord, [who expect, look for, and hope in Him], shall change and renew their strength and power; they shall lift their wings and mount up [close to God] as eagles [mount up to the sun]; they shall run and not be weary, they shall walk and not faint or become tired.**
>
> **Isaiah 40:28-31** AMP

Actually, if you'll study the Hebrew meaning behind the phrase "change and renew their strength," as used in that passage, you'll find it is speaking of an *exchange* of strength. In other words, when you wait on God, you exchange your human strength for His divine strength.

That's a good deal because God's strength and power do not fluctuate. He's always omnipotent. His strength never diminishes. Contrary to some silly, traditional ideas, God is not a doddering old man. We don't call Him "Rock of Ages" because He's old. Some people picture God as having this long white beard, because they think He's aging. No, God is not old, and He doesn't lack any strength.

He is the God of all strength. In the passage we just read, Isaiah said that even young people faint and grow weary. But Isaiah says that God can give us strength that is beyond human vigor, beyond human vitality. We would call this a spiritual quickening or a spiritual renewing.

Who is going to receive this renewal of strength? Those who rush around? Those who are so busy that they don't have time to even sit down? No, *those who wait on the Lord* will renew their strength. (v. 31.)

Be Still

I have found in my own life that *wait* is one word that the flesh does not care for very much. The flesh likes the word *go*. Isn't that the truth?

The technology that we see today did not exist in Jesus' day. When He went from Jericho to Jerusalem, He didn't drive a car;

He walked. So if it took Him all day to walk to one destination, He must have stopped and rested. Not only did Jesus rest His physical body, but there were also times when He was still and He waited on the Lord. There were times of reflection in His life and ministry.

Have you found that even when you are lying down in bed, your mind still could be going 100 miles an hour? That's not real rest.

The Bible said to wait upon the Lord. You cannot truly wait on the Lord if your mind is not at rest. You must be still before Him. Psalm 46:10 says, *Be still*, **and know that I am God.** Psalm 4:4 says, **Stand in awe, and sin not: commune with your own heart upon your bed, and** *be still.*

Do you know that the Lord will talk to you if you will just sit quietly before Him? He likes to talk to you. Many of us just do not ever get quiet enough for Him to talk to us.

In my experience with Him, I have actually found Him to be kind of a motor-mouth. I remember one day, He talked to me so much that I could have written a whole book. At one point the telephone rang, and I said to Him, "You'll just have to excuse me." I felt so rude for interrupting Him.

God loves it when His people wait on Him. Allow your spirit to receive from God in quiet times like this. Turn your mind off, get your heart centered on God and yield to the Spirit of God in these times.

You should not allow your spirit to get anxious in times of waiting. You should not allow your flesh to overtake you and say, *Well, what are we doing next?*

Spend Time Beholding Him

The most spiritual people I know are people who meditate on the Word of God.

Some people think the word *meditate* means sitting in the corner somewhere, cross-legged, chanting something weird. But Jesus wrote the book on meditation, and that is not the way He defines it. Meditation on God is setting your thoughts on Him, waiting on Him. It is turning your heart toward Him and keeping your heart there.

Somebody once told me, "Spend time beholding Him." That's what waiting on the Lord is—spending time beholding Him. Get by yourself, get quiet and fellowship with the Lord. Wait on the Lord.

Let God Talk for a Change

When we spend time listening to God's words, they will sustain us and strengthen our spirits, souls and bodies. Jesus said, **Man shall not live by bread alone, but by every word of God** (Luke 4:4). We live by the words God speaks. Jesus said that, and He also lived it. He lived by God's words proceeding to Him and flowing through Him.

Lazarus, Come Forth!

We can see this in the story of Lazarus in John 11. We know that Lazarus died and Jesus raised him from the dead; but before

Jesus performed this miracle, some very important things happened that help us understand the way in which Jesus raised Lazarus from the dead.

Starting in verse 1, we see that Lazarus and his sisters, Mary and Martha, lived in the village of Bethany in Jordan. (Mary was the one who anointed the Lord with perfume and wiped His feet with her hair.) Lazarus was ill, so his sisters sent word to the Lord that the one whom He loved was sick. (vv. 1-3.)

Now Jesus had departed from Judaea because the Jews there had tried to kill Him, so it was not wise at this time for Him to go to Bethany. Yet, we knew that when Jesus heard that His friend in Bethany needed Him, he must have wanted to go there.

In fact, we are told very directly in John 11:5 AMP that **Jesus loved Martha and her sister and Lazarus. [They were His dear friends, and He held them in loving esteem.]** Don't you know that He wanted to go to them immediately when He heard Lazarus was sick?

But He didn't because He was living off the words proceeding from the mouth of God. Therefore, verse 6 says, even when He heard that Lazarus was sick, He stayed where He was two more days. What was He doing there? He was waiting for God to say, *Go.*

Then after that interval, He said to His disciples, "Let's go back to Judaea." (v. 7.) Now, remember we just read that they were seeking to kill Him in Judaea. It was not safe for Him to travel there. But He said, "We're going back to Judaea."

The disciples argued with Him. "The Jews there just tried to stone and kill You, and You want to go back?" they asked in disbelief.

> **Jesus answered, Are there not twelve hours in the day? Anyone who walks about in the daytime does not stumble, because he sees [by] the light of this world. But if anyone walks about in the night, he does stumble, because there is no light in him [the light is lacking to him].**
>
> **He said these things, and then added, Our friend Lazarus is at rest and sleeping; but I am going there that I may awaken him out of his sleep.**
>
> **The disciples answered, Lord, if he is sleeping, he will recover.**
>
> **However, Jesus had spoken of his death, but they thought He referred to falling into a refreshing and natural sleep.**
>
> **So then Jesus told them plainly, Lazarus is dead.**
>
> **John 11:9-14** AMP

How did He know Lazarus was dead? The sisters had only told Him that Lazarus was sick. He hadn't gone to Bethany to find out how he was. So when did He find out Lazarus was dead?

While He was waiting on the Lord.

Notice what He said in verse 9: **Are there not twelve hours in the day? Anyone who walks about in the daytime does not stumble, because he sees [by] the light.** What light was He talking about? The sunshine? No, He was talking about being led by the light of the words proceeding from the mouth of God.

He was saying, "If I walk by My Father's words, I'm not going to stumble and fall. I've heard God speaking to Me, telling Me to go; therefore, I will go."

And when He *did* go, not only did He have the *words* that were proceeding from God, but He also had the power. Why? The Word and the power go together. The Word and the Spirit are one. Jesus moved right along by the Word and the Spirit of God; therefore, God's power in Him protected Him in Bethany and restored a dead man to life.

God's Words Bring Peace

Jeremiah is another example of one who learned to be led by the words proceeding from the mouth of the Lord. Look at Jeremiah 15:17-18 AMP:

> **I sat not in the assembly of those who make merry, nor did I rejoice; I sat alone.... Why is my pain perpetual and my wound incurable, refusing to be healed? Will you indeed be to me a deceitful brook, like waters that fail and are uncertain?**

Jeremiah's mind was troubled and restless. He was in a terrible situation. But when he chose to wait on and listen to the Lord, this is what God said to him:

> **If you return [and give up this mistaken tone of distrust and despair], then I will give to you again a settled place of quiet and safety, and you will be My minister; and if you separate the precious from the vile [cleansing your own heart from unworthy and unwar-**

ranted suspicions concerning God's faithfulness], you shall be My mouthpiece.... I will make you to this people a fortified, bronze wall.

Jeremiah 15:19,20 AMP

Jeremiah was frequently in a posture of quietly waiting on the Lord. Therefore, he often heard the Lord's voice. In verse 16, Jeremiah said, **Thy words were found, and I did eat them; and thy word was unto me the joy and rejoicing of mine heart: for I am called by thy name, O Lord God of hosts.** Because he ate the words that were proceeding out of the mouth of God in his time of waiting, he found out who God is. He discovered that God is a God of peace.

Get Thee Behind Me, Satan!

One major characteristic of the Devil is restlessness. Jesus said that when an unclean spirit goes out of a man, it goes through dry places seeking rest but can't find it. (Luke 11:24.) Have you ever noticed that anyone who is extremely oppressed of the Devil cannot sit still? They're always going and going and going.

But God is called the God of peace. He never gets in a rush. If we want His peace in our lives, we must be still and rest in His presence, listening for His voice. Jesus, our example, showed us how to do this, even in the midst of trials and tests. Let's look at Luke 4:1-8 AMP:

Then Jesus, full of and controlled by the Holy Spirit, returned from the Jordan and was led in [by] the [Holy] Spirit for (during) forty days in the wilderness (desert), where He was tempted (tried, tested exceedingly) by the

Devil. And He ate nothing during those days, and when they were completed, He was hungry.

Then the Devil said to Him, If You are the Son of God, order this stone to turn into a loaf [of bread].

And Jesus replied to him, It is written, Man shall not live by bread alone but by every word and expression of God.

Then the Devil took Him up to a high mountain and showed Him all the kingdoms of the habitable world in a moment of time [in the twinkling of an eye]. And he said to Him, To You I will give all this power and authority and their glory for it has been turned over to me, and I give it to whomever I will. Therefore if You will do homage to and worship me [just once], it shall all be Yours.

And Jesus replied to him, *Get behind Me, Satan!* It is written, You shall...worship the Lord your God, and Him only shall you serve.

So Jesus, full of the Holy Ghost, returned from the Jordan and was led by the Spirit into the wilderness.

Now, I see one thing for sure. I see a power, a might, a glory and a majesty falling on Jesus to the point that He wasn't even the same man. He received a mighty anointing from God, and the only thing that He could do was just submit to it and yield to it. So He submitted and yielded, and the more He did so, the more He was covered by God's power and led by the Spirit.

The Holy Ghost took Him away into the wilderness, where He experienced much darkness and loneliness. He went for forty days without food, so His body was weak; and His situation was getting continually worse.

But Jesus knew that within human inability God finds His opportunity. He knew the power of God was going to take Him through. He knew the anointing that came from His yielding to the words proceeding from the mouth of God would take Him through any crisis.

Don't you know God the Father was saying to Jesus, "Just let Me at him. Just yield; just submit to the Holy Ghost. Just let Me at him. Don't *You* get at him; just let *Me* at him!" So when Jesus finally had to deal with Satan, He said, "It is written," backed by the authority of God Himself and with a power strong enough to rip Satan to shreds.

Throughout the Gospels, we see that the way Jesus won every victory was by hearing the words that proceed from the mouth of God, yielding to the power of God and letting God do what He wanted to do.

Revelation on an Uninhabited Island

Do you remember the great apostle John, the writer of the book of Revelation? John was the disciple who leaned on Jesus' breast at the Last Supper. He called himself the disciple that Jesus loved. John knew how to wait on the Lord. That waiting made him so strong that the enemies of God gnashed their teeth at John as he went throughout the country. They did everything they could to destroy him. Some of the commentaries say that they even boiled him in oil, but no matter what they did, they could not harm him. He just slipped right on by.

So they said, "That does it. We're going to stick him over there on the Isle of Patmos. That should be the end of him."

That should have been the end of him, but in Revelation 1 we read that on the island he was in the Spirit on the Lord's day. The very place that was not fit for humanity was the very place that John was the most filled with God's thoughts. God anointed him with power, just as He had anointed Jesus and Jeremiah when they had listened for His voice in their times alone with Him.

We Must Yield

And so it can be for us. Do you know that is how you got saved? You heard words proceeding from the mouth of God, you yielded to those words, and the power of God changed your inner man.

That's the way you got baptized in the Holy Ghost. You heard words proceeding from the mouth of God, you yielded and submitted to those words and the power of God came.

That is how you will receive your healing. If you will hear the words proceeding from the mouth of God and yield to those words, then the power of God will heal your body.

Remember, there is nothing you cannot walk through. There is nothing too hard for God to take you through, if you yield to the power of the Spirit and to the words proceeding from His mouth.

We need to wait on the Spirit of the Lord and rest in His presence. We need to allow heaven's resources to come to us.

No matter how rocky and desolate the isle, no matter how barren the wilderness, no matter how unfriendly the place, be filled with God. Give Him full control. Then you will find yourself living in the Spirit. You will find your times of human inability will be His opportunities to display His omnipotence. You will find you will be in the right place at the right time. You will find every need met as you rest in God's presence, listen for His voice and yield to the Holy Ghost's power every day.

Chapter 5

Your *Prescription* for
Divine Health

My son, attend to my words; consent and submit to my sayings. Let them not depart from your sight; keep them in the center of your heart. For they are life unto those who find them, healing and health to all their flesh. Keep and guard your heart with all vigilance and above all that you guard, for out of it flow the springs of life.

Proverbs 4:20-23 AMP

Notice this Scripture passage says to attend to the Word of God, to incline your ear unto it with an enshrining heart. We need to look unto the Word of God until the manifestation of our healing, or whatever we are believing for, comes to pass.

In the twenty-eight years that my husband and I have been walking with the Lord, we have found that this Scripture is true and it works.

No matter what the Devil tried to throw in our faces, no matter what came our way, if we would attend to the Word of God, incline our ears unto it and submit unto its sayings, God would work a miracle and give us life in our area of need.

Some terrible things have happened to us. One time the Devil told me that I was going blind. When I went to the doctor, I found out I was within three months of total blindness. Now, that is what you call an attack of the Devil. It was a lie from the Devil, from the pit of hell.

That was the Devil's report. God's report, though, was that Jesus delivered me. At Calvary, I was healed.

So what did I do? Just as Proverbs 4:20-21 instructed me, I got busy attending to the Word of God. I did not let it depart from my eyes. I inclined my ear to it. I kept it in the midst of my heart. And just as verse 22 says, when I found the Word of God, it brought me life and health and healing and wholeness.

Hit the Wall

Have you ever watched swimmers doing laps in a pool? They jump into the water and start swimming; but when they get to the end of the pool, they can go no farther.

Sometimes in life, you find yourself in situations like that—where you have hit the end and can go no further in your own strength.

But what do those swimmers do? They hit the wall. They kick off from that wall, and that wall becomes a boost to them. It pushes them off.

The Word of God can become that to you. It can just flat cheer you on. Sometimes people face situations that would normally break, kill or at least embitter a person. Yet the people who are full of the Word of God will come through them and just end up being more like Jesus. Now, understand that attacks of the Devil do not make them more like Jesus. The Word of God is what pushes them on to victory. When you are full of the Word, that Word will do wonderful, marvelous things.

Some Christians are full of God's Word, but others have what I call "slim pickings." You can *have* the truth and not be full of the truth. You can be a Christian and say, "I love Jesus," yet not *be full* of His love or power. When you are truly full of the Word of God, though, it will take you through to victory every time. It will enable you to receive from God the healing and deliverance you need.

Locked in the Stall

I remember one particular time when being full of the Word brought me through a very peculiar situation. The day that it happened, I was preparing for a prayer leaders' Christmas party that would be at my house later that night. I only had a few things left to do before the party, so I thought I'd whip into K-Mart and get a little shopping done.

Well, I knew when I hit that parking lot that I was transgressing my heart. Have you ever known you were not supposed to do something but did it anyway? Well, I knew I shouldn't go into K-Mart, but I went on in anyway.

I got my cart and pushed my way through. After paying for my items, I decided to go to the ladies' room before leaving. I took all of my purchases into the stall, and do you know what happened to me? The lock jammed!

In the ladies' bathroom of K-Mart, I was standing bewildered. I thought, *Devil, if you think I'm going to spend the afternoon in the bathroom stall at K-Mart, you are wrong!*

About that time a lady came through the door. I could see through the crack that she was an employee. So I told her the door was jammed and asked her to go get the security officer to open the door of the stall.

So that lady left—and never came back! I mean she really left!

About five minutes later, another lady came into the stall next to mine.

I told her what had happened. And she said, "Ohhhhh, I wish I could help you." And that was the end of the conversation.

Normally I would have crawled underneath the stall door, but these doors were built unusually low—only a few inches from the floor—so no one could crawl under.

I began to encourage myself. *I'll be just fine, just fine,* I thought.

Stand Up, Speak Up and Fight

I remembered a message I had heard one time about speaking to the "its" in our lives. The message was about the time when Jesus saw the unfruitful fig tree and spoke to it, and it obeyed His command to wither away. (Matt. 21:19.) Jesus said, **If ye have faith, and doubt not, ye shall not only do this which is done to the fig tree, but also if ye shall say unto this mountain, Be thou removed, and be thou cast into the sea; it shall be done** (v. 21).

This lock was an *it*. All of a sudden, the Word that was in me started to rise up. That lady was still in the next stall, but that Word rose up in my life right there—and the power of God hit me.

I said, "In the name of Jesus, door, you come open!" Then I kicked it with my foot and hit it with my arm, and do you know what happened? That door came open, and I sailed out of that bathroom!

As I was leaving, that lady who had been in the stall next to mine saw me. Her eyes were huge! She was pushing her cart, and she almost ran it into the wall looking at me.

You know, some Christians give up anytime the least little thing hits them. They just fall out somewhere. However, people who are full of the Word of God don't just lie down; they stand up, speak up and fight for their rights in Christ.

Don't Be Like the Opossums

My grandfather had a plantation when I was young. Every summer we would go out there and stay all summer long. On his plantation, there were so many opossums.

As children, we used to like to watch the opossums out there. They walked funny. They didn't really watch where they were going, but kept their heads down and just stumbled into whatever was in front of them.

They were senseless little creatures. I believe God created them as a private joke at the end of the third day. We would watch those opossums cross the road and just laugh forever at those little creatures. They would dart across the street and not even look. They just moved along, went right into the curb and keeled over.

The Word will get you over life's bumps, large and small. But some Christians are like those opossums. They just hit one small thing, and instead of letting it boost them into the Word of God, they just fall over somewhere. For instance, when they start to feel some symptoms of sickness, instead of looking to the Word on healing, they accept those symptoms and say, "I'm sick."

But the Bible says you have to be full of the Word of God. You have to stay full of it. And then out of the abundance of what you are full of, that is what you will live by. That is what you will speak when symptoms attack your body: "By Jesus' stripes, I am healed."

Out of the Abundance of the Heart

The other day I was talking to a young lady who was overcoming cancer. As we were talking, I was really trying to locate where she was in faith. About halfway through the conversation, she realized that she had made many bad confessions during the conversation, so she started backtracking.

It occurred to me that if you are always having to watch your confession, you are not full of the Word of God. Matthew 12:34 says, **Out of the abundance of the heart the mouth speaketh.** When your heart is full of the Word of God, confessing it becomes second nature for you. It is not something that you're striving to do. It is just what you do.

Healing for the Whole Person

Now, we read in Proverbs 4:23 that God's words are **life unto those that find them, and health to all their flesh.** This health that God promises applies not only to your flesh, but to every part of your life. Joshua 1:8, a similar passage, says, **This book of the law shall not depart out of thy mouth; but thou shalt meditate therein day and night...for then thou shalt make thy way prosperous, and then thou shalt have good success.**

If you meditate on the Word of God, your whole being will be successful. If you meditate on the Word, if you submit to it, if you let it not depart from your sight, if you keep it in the center of your heart, it will be life for everything.

These Scriptures right here give us the divine method of receiving the blessings that God has already provided for us in Christ Jesus. God has already provided everything we need. According to Psalm 4:20-23 and Joshua 1:8, the only thing we must do to receive His life is to make God's Word our priority.

It matters not which part of you is dysfunctional or which part of you is unhealthy. It could be your brain, your legs, your heart, your liver. It could even be any of the affairs of life, any situation. It could be poverty or lack.

Is poverty or lack trying to come on you? Is sickness attacking your body? Is depression bombarding your mind? Submit to the Word and live out of the Word. If you'll attend to it with an absolute enshrining heart and go after it, you'll find out the Word will work for you. It will bring life to your whole being and to every situation.

Instead of having your eyes on your problem, instead of being occupied with your symptoms or the situation, you must keep your eyes on the Word. **My son,** *attend* **to my words,** Proverbs 4:20 says.

That word *attend* is the Hebrew word *qashab,* and it means "to hearken, give heed to or regard."[1] You're not giving heed to the Word of God when it sits on your nightstand gathering dust!

We must attend or give heed to God's Word continually. It must be before our eyes each day. We must be occupied with and influenced only by what the Word of God says. You see, when we give heed to the Word of God, we expect things to change and come into agreement with God's Word.

A Snake *on a Stick?*

This principle of gazing upon the promise of the Lord is illustrated very clearly in the book of Numbers.

The Israelites began to complain against Moses and against the Lord, and thus they opened the door for an attack to come upon them. Fiery serpents came and bit them.

Just as the Israelites were bitten by snakes, you and I have been bitten by the serpent, the Devil. But there is a way to survive the bites of the serpent. Numbers 21:7-8 AMP says:

> **And the people came to Moses, and said, We have sinned, for we have spoken against the Lord and against you; pray to the Lord, that He may take away the**

serpents from us. So Moses prayed for the people. And the Lord said to Moses, Make a fiery serpent [of bronze] and set it on a pole; and everyone who is bitten, when he *looks* at it, shall live.

Everyone who looked at—not *glanced at it*—everyone who was occupied with, influenced by, gazing at, staring at the bronze serpent would live.

That word was the promise unto them. It was an amazing promise. It may have even sounded like a crazy promise. Suppose God told you to go stare at a pole if you were sick. What if God told you to put a serpent on the pole and stare at it until you were healed? How would that set with you?

But that was the promise here. That was what they had to do. They had to attend to that Word. So Moses made a serpent of the bronze and put it on the pole. Then when any man who had been bitten by a serpent looked at that serpent on a pole, he lived.

In other words, he was forgiven, and he was healed.

> **And Moses made a serpent of bronze and put it on a pole, and if a serpent had bitten any man, when he looked to the serpent of bronze [attentively, expectantly, with a steady and absorbing gaze], he lived.**
>
> **Numbers 21:9 AMP**

That was the condition. They had to look at the promise. They had to look at what God had provided, and then they lived.

Look Upon Jesus

Jesus applied this very Scripture to Himself.

And as Moses lifted up the serpent in the wilderness, even so must the Son of Man be lifted up.

John 3:14

He was saying that the Scripture in Numbers is an Old Testament type of the work of Calvary. If you will look steadfastly and expectantly, be occupied with and influenced by Calvary and the work of redemption, God will perform every promise in the Bible for *you*. He will redeem your spirit, heal your body, provide for your every need and give you all the desires of your heart.

Abraham Looked at the Promise

You can see how well this principle works by looking at the life of Abraham. When God told him he was going to have a child, in the natural it looked impossible. He was an old man. Romans 4:19 AMP speaks of **the [utter] impotence of his own body, which was as good as dead because he was about a hundred years old.** And Sarah was an old, barren woman with a "deadened womb," Romans 4:19 says.

There was no way Abraham could be the father of a child, much less many nations. (Gen. 17:4.)

However, God made a promise to him. That promise is recorded in Genesis 17:5: **I have made you a father of many nations.** That's what God said to Abraham. At that very moment, the promise was true in the eyes of God. It was done; it was finished.

Even so, there was no human reason why Abraham should believe that promise. He couldn't see it. It was the furthest thing away from a possibility that he had ever heard of. But we are told, **Abraham...hope being gone, hoped in faith that he should become the father of many nations, just as he had been promised** (Rom. 4:18 AMP).

He did not weaken in faith when he considered the [utter] impotence of his own body, which was as good as dead because he was about a hundred years old (v. 19 AMP). In other words, he wasn't being occupied with what his eyes saw. He wasn't attending to the limitations of his body.

Nor did he consider the barrenness of Sarah's womb. He didn't even consider it. Abraham walked in faith. He looked beyond the problem and looked unto God's promise. He became a doer of Proverbs 4:20-21. He attended to God's words; he didn't let them depart from his eyes; he kept them enshrined in his heart. He didn't even think of anything except God's promise that he would be the father of many nations.

> **No unbelief or distrust made him waver (doubtingly question) concerning the promise of God, but he grew strong and was empowered by faith as he gave praise and glory to God, fully satisfied and assured that God was able and mighty to keep His Word and to do what He had promised.**
>
> **Romans 4:20,21 AMP**

These two verses sum up Abraham's faith and God's response to his faith. Abraham looked unto and believed God's promise unwaveringly, and God mightily fulfilled his promise. Abraham did, indeed, become the father of many nations.

Set Your Eyes on the Word

Now, some Christians' faith would be summed up this way: "Their faith waxed weaker and weaker while they looked unto their circumstances and forgot the promise. Unbelief, distrust and doubtful wavering caused them to question the promise. And they grew more and more helpless and fearful and were empowered with death because of it, fully assured that God was just unable to keep His Word or to do what He had promised."

But you see, that is not what Abraham did. Abraham held to the promise. God is no respecter of persons. (Col. 3:25.) If, like Abraham, you will believe Him, set your eyes on His Word and look to His promise, then God is able and will do what He has promised you. He will heal, deliver and prosper you.

God's Promises Are Seeds

The Word of God is so mighty—every word of it. Some Christians look at the Word as if it were just another book. They see words written on a page, which carry about that much weight in their lives—just words on a page. But these words are different words. These words are containers of the power of almighty God.

We can look at it like this. The Bible says that the Word of God is seed. Envision a very small seed growing into a large plant. You may look at the plant later and say, "How was that plant in this tiny seed?"

God says that His Word is power. It has life in it, just as a seed has a plant in it. Promises are like seeds. They may seem pretty powerless when they are in the seed stage, but if you will plant them inside of you and attend to them, they will manifest in a powerful way.

What happens to you when you put the Word in your heart? It conceives, and it brings forth. That is how Abraham brought forth the seed Isaac. He brought him forth by the power of God.

Attack the Symptom Weeds With the Word

Now, God's promise to Abraham become reality the moment Abraham believed it. At that moment it was done. It took some time, however, for the natural circumstances to change.

That's usually the way it is. The moment you believe for healing, God's power goes to work destroying that sickness at the root. But for a while things don't look much different.

I thought about that one summer. I seemed to have extra weeds in my yard, so I got out my little squirt bottle of weed killer and went around my yard spraying, spraying, spraying. As I squirted each weed, in my mind's eye, that weed was dead. It did not look dead in the natural. In fact, it was still giving evidence of life.

But twenty-four hours later, I went back to my yard, and every one of those weeds was brown and crispy. That weed killer took care of it.

This is exactly how the promises of God work. When you are believing for healing, you take the sword of the Spirit, you attend to the promises of God and you use it to attack the sickness.

And just like the weed killer, the Word starts attacking that sickness the minute you start attending to it and looking at it. Now, those symptom weeds may linger for a while. But with your mind's eye, you can see them gone and your body made completely whole.

I Got It!

In 1978, I was preaching up in Wilmer, Minnesota. Right in the middle of the message, a little girl about midway to the back stood up and started yelling, "I got it! I got it! I got it!"

I knew exactly what she meant, because I had experienced that same joy when God's promises became revelation to me.

There was a day when I was believing God for healing in my body. I was a basket case. I had bleeding stomach ulcers that the doctors could not control no matter what they tried. I was throwing up all night, and I had chronic depression at the same time.

Then I started attending to the Word. I started inclining my ear unto what it said. I started not letting it depart from my eyes.

I just did it, day after day after day. That is what you have to do. Just keep attending to the Word. *Well, how long do I have to do that?* you may be wondering. You keep inclining your ears, your eyes and your heart to the Word till you get healed, till you see your manifestation, till you see things change.

As I attended to God's Word, it became life to my flesh. My entire being was flooded with His life, and I knew sickness had to leave. Everything within me shouted, *I got it! I got it! I got it!*

You see, when that girl said, "I got it!" the Word of God dropped from being information in her head and entered her heart. There's a lot of difference between processing information and conceiving the Word in your heart.

Mary's Promise

The most wonderful example we have of what can happen when the Word of God is conceived in the heart and is allowed by faith to bring forth its fruit is seen in the life of Mary, the mother of Jesus. She was just a little virgin Israeli girl, yet God spoke the most amazing Word to her. He sent an angelic messenger and said:

> **Do not be afraid, Mary, for you have found grace (free, spontaneous, absolute favor and loving-kindness) with God. And listen! You will become pregnant and will give birth to a Son, and you shall call His name Jesus.**
>
> **He will be great (eminent) and will be called the Son of the Most High; and the Lord will give to Him the**

throne of His forefather David, and He will reign over the house of Jacob throughout the ages; and of His reign there will be no end.

And Mary said to the angel, How can this be, since I have no [intimacy with any man as a] husband?

Then the angel said to her, The Holy Spirit will come upon you, and the power of the Most High will overshadow you [like a shining cloud]; and so the holy (pure, sinless) Thing (Offspring) which shall be born *of you* will be called the Son of God.

And listen! Your relative Elizabeth in her old age has also conceived a son, and this is now the sixth month with her who was called barren. For with God nothing is ever impossible and no word from God shall be without power or impossible of fulfillment.

Luke 1:30-37 AMP

No word from God is without power or impossible of fulfillment. Not even this promise, which looked absolutely infeasible, was impossible with God. I mean, look at what it says. The angel came to Mary, a virgin, and told her she would bear a child.

Do you think she understood that word? Sometimes people want to understand everything before they will believe. Do you think she understood that the Holy Spirit was going to come on her and the power of the Most High would overshadow her? With her mind, she could not possibly have understood this promise from God. But she said, **Be it unto me according to thy word** (Luke 1:38).

Mary heard the Word, attended to it, looked to it, conceived it in her heart, conceived it in her body and brought it forth. And we do exactly the same thing.

Mary became occupied with the Word of God. Not according to the impossibility of it, not according to the situation, but simply *according to God's Word* Mary conceived and gave birth to the Messiah.

Not Just *the* Healer; *My* Healer

It is amazing what can happen when people get the Word down on the inside of them. I know that Jesus is *the* healer. But there was a day when the promise of God dropped into my heart that He was *my* healer. It didn't do me much good to know that Jesus is the healer. Until Jesus became *my* healer, it really didn't matter.

I vividly remember the day when it dropped down on the inside of me because I had attended to the Word and because I had not let it depart from my eyes. I had kept it in the center of my heart, and I had inclined unto it with my ears.

I remember the day Jesus became *my* provider. Oh, brother or sister, it's wonderful that He's your provider. But I've got to know that He's *my* provider.

I'm telling you, the Word of the living God is true, and its promises manifest for every person who will attend to it, who will look to it, who will gaze upon it with a steadfast and gripping look, who will become occupied and influenced by it and who will expect that what God has promised, He will assuredly do.

Be a Doer of the Word

He will fulfill His Word in your life. The secret is in your doing the Word. The Bible says that you're not going to get blessed just because you read this Book. The Bible says that not only must you hear the Word, but you must also become doers of the Word. (James 1:23.)

If you will set your heart, set all the faculties of your being, to do the Word—to do what it says, to attend to it, to let it not depart from your eyes, to keep it in the midst of your heart, to incline your ear unto what it says—then it will be life, health and healing to you.

It will change situations. It doesn't matter what has happened to you, where you came from or what your past looked like. The Word of God is the power of God unto you.

My Prayer for You

I am going to pray a prayer for you now.

"Father, you know that my desire for this reader is that he or she would hear, receive and believe the promise that You have given, knowing without a doubt that You are able to perform it, in the name of Jesus.

"Father, even before the hosts of heaven and the demons of hell, I thank You this day that when Jesus comes, this reader will be found in Him, full of the Word of God, in strength and in joy, soberness and vigilance, in the name of Jesus. Amen."

Endnotes

Chapter 1
[1]Strong, "Hebrew," entry #2483, p. 39.'
[2]Brown et al., s.v. "borne," entry #5375, p. 669.
[3]Strong, "Hebrew," entry #4341, p. 66.
[4]Vaughan.
[5]Leeser.
[6]Vaughan.

Chapter 5
[1]Strong, "Hebrew," entry #7181, p. 105.

References

Brown, Francis D.D., Litt.; S.R. Driver, D.D., Litt. D. and Charles A. Briggs, D.D.,D. Litt. Peabody: Hendrickson Publishers, 1997.

Leeser, Isaac. *Twenty-Four Books of the Holy Scriptures.* New York: Hebrew Publishing Company, 1998.

Strong, James. *Strong's Exhaustive Concordance of the Bible.* "Hebrew and Chaldee Dictionary," "Greek Dictionary of the New Testament." Nashville: Abingdon, 1978.

Vaughan, Curtis, Th.D., Ed. *The Word: The Bible From 26 Translations.* Moss Point: Mathis Publishers, Inc., 1993.

About the Author

Lynne Hammond is a nationally known teacher and writer on the subject of prayer. Her books include *Dare To Be Free* and *The Master Is Calling: Discovering the Wonders of Spirit-Led Prayer.*

She is the host and teacher for *A Call to Prayer,* a weekly European television broadcast, and is an occasional guest teacher on *The Winner's Way With Mac Hammond,* a national weekly television broadcast. She also writes regular articles on the subject of prayer in *Winner's Way* magazine and publishes a quarterly newsletter called *Prayer Notes* for people of prayer. Lynne is a frequent speaker at national prayer conferences and meetings around the country.

Lynne's husband, Mac, is founder and pastor of Living Word Christian Center, a large and growing church in Minneapolis, Minnesota. Under Lynne's leadership, the prayer ministry at Living Word has become a nationally recognized model for developing effective "pray-ers"—the phrase Lynne has coined—in the local church.

The desire of Lynne's heart is to impart the spirit of prayer to churches and nations throughout the world.

To contact Lynne Hammond,
write

Mac Hammond Ministries
P.O. Box 29469
Minneapolis, MN 55429

Please include your prayer requests
and comments when you write.

Other Books by Lynne Hammond

Dare To Be Free!

The Master Is Calling:
Discovering the Wonders of Spirit-Led Prayer

Available from your local bookstore.

Harrison House
Tulsa, Oklahoma 74153

The Harrison House Vision

Proclaiming the truth and the power

Of the Gospel of Jesus Christ

With excellence;

Challenging Christians to

Live victoriously,

Grow spiritually,

Know God intimately.